Cool Ca

Written by John Foster

Contents

Collins

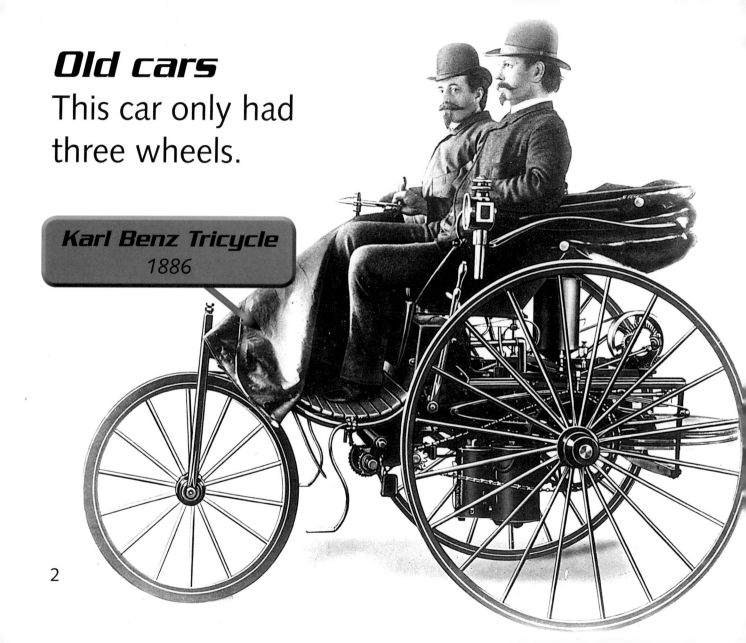

Old cars

This car only had three wheels.

Karl Benz Tricycle
1886

2

This car had a top speed of
12 kilometres per hour.

Salvesen Steam Cart
1896

Fast cars

These cars can go at more than 400 kilometres per hour.

Ultimate Aero
top speed: 410 kilometres per hour

Bugatti Veyron
top speed: 430 kilometres per hour

This car goes so fast that it has a parachute to slow it down so it can stop safely.

"Vampire" Jet dragster

Racing cars and bangers

These cars race at more than
300 kilometres per hour.

Formula One racing cars

There are many crashes when bangers race.

Rare cars

Some cars cost a lot of money to make. Only five of these cars are being made.

Bugatti Veyron
16.4 Super Sport World Record Edition

This car is covered with crystals.

Mercedes SL600
with 300,000 crystals

Flying cars and floating cars

This car has wings and can fly.

The Python

This car can travel on water.

Odd cars

This car is only 55 centimetres tall.

The Flat Out

This car is used in an advert for shoes.

electric shoe car

Cool cars: unique features

Karl Benz Tricycle

3 wheels

Salvesen Steam Cart

top speed
12 miles per hour

Ultimate Aero

top speed 410
kilometres per hour

Bugatti Veyron Super Sport

only five made

Mercedes SL600

covered in crystals

Flying Car

has wings and
can fly

Bugatti Veyron

top speed 430
kilometres per hour

"Vampire" Jet Dragster

parachute slows
it down

Formula One Racing Cars

race at more than
300 kilometres
per hour

Bangers

crash when
they race

The Python

travels on water

The Flat Out

only 55
centimetres tall

Electric Shoe Car

an advert
for shoes

Ideas for reading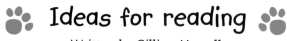

Written by Gillian Howell
Primary Literacy Consultant

Learning objectives: *(reading objectives correspond with Yellow band; all other objectives correspond with Copper band)* use phonics to read unknown or difficult words, including the full range of digraphs to decode unknown words; identify and make notes of the main points of sections of text; follow up on others' points to show whether they agree or disagree; use layout, format, graphics, illustrations for different purposes

Curriculum links: Design and Technology: Vehicles; Science: Forces and movement

High frequency words: old, had, three, this, had, a, of, these, can, go, at, more, than, so, that, it, has, to, down, one, there, are, many, when, some, make, five, made, with, and, on, is, as, an, for

Interest words: kilometres, wheels, Bugatti, parachute, bangers, crystals, flying, floating, centimetres

Resources: paper, pens, pencils

Word count: 165

Getting started

- Read the title together and look at the front cover. Ask the children what first impression the cover photograph gives. Ask them if anyone has ever seen a car like this and what they think of it.

- Prompt the children to suggest what sort of information they might find out in this book. Ask the children to discuss the types of cars they will be reading about with a partner. Do they know anything about the cars described in the blurb?

- Ask the children to read the contents page aloud. If children struggle with any of the words, for example, *floating* or *special,* remind them to break the words into sounds and then run them together again. Prompt the children to pronounce the *c* in *special* as *sh*.

- Ask the children in pairs to choose a chapter from the contents page and read it together. Ask them to make notes of key facts to report back to the group.

Reading and responding

- Ask the children to read their chosen chapters using a quiet voice. Listen to the children as they read and prompt as necessary.

- On p4, point out the captions in the photograph. Ask the children to attempt the words in the